S T R I V E N

THE BRIGHT TREATISE

STRIVEN
THE BRIGHT TREATISE

JEFFREY PETHYBRIDGE

NOEMI PRESS
LAS CRUCES, NEW MEXICO

Noemi Press
P.O. Box 1330
Mesilla Park, NM 88047
www.noemipress.org

STRIVEN, THE BRIGHT TREATISE

Image credit (p. 49): *Dante and Virgil before Pier della Vigna* (1861) by Gustave Doré

LIBRARY OF CONGRESS CATALOGING-IN-PUBLICATION DATA
Pethybridge, Jeffrey.
[Poems. Selections]
Striven, the bright treatise / Jeffrey Pethybridge .
Includes index.
Poems.
ISBN 978-1-934819-29-6
I. Title.
PS3616.E849S77 2013
811'.6--dc23

Published by Noemi Press, a nonprofit literary organization
www.noemipress.org

In memory of my brother Tad Pethybridge
(4 February 1962 – 7 January 2007)

ACKNOWLEDGMENTS

Sincere thanks to editors of the following journals, in which versions of these poems first appeared: *32 Poems*: "Lower Limit Song, The Chord" | *Borderlands:* "Four Brothers," "Good Bye O Sun" | *Cellpoems*: lines 1-32 from "The Book of Lamps" | *Crazyhorse*: "Twenty Thousand Songs" | *Grist* : "Written in Grease-Pencil on a Large Mirror" | *Indefinite Space*: "The New Humors (1)" and "The New Humors (2)" | *The Iowa Review*: "The Sword of Ajax: A Report on Democracy and Soldier Suicides" | LIT: "The Railing / The Loom" and "Alighieri's God Is Not Great" | *Modern Language Studies:* "Through Me You Enter" | *New American Writing*: "Zone" | *New Orleans Review*: "Arming-Theme" | *Notre Dame Review*: "Poem Spoken to the Air," "'The Fire of Culture,'" and "Grief-Debt" | PANK: "Two Consecutive Pages in a Notebook," "[In the dream where the telephone call]," and "The Father of Suicidology" | *Poor Claudia*: "Against Suicide," "Fathom-Line," and lines 33-64 from "The Book of Lamps" | *Puerto del Sol*: "The Chronicle of the King of the Lonely Grave" | *Unstuck*: "Aokigahara" | *Washington Square*: "The House After The Forest & The Fever."

"Lower Limit Song, The Chord" is reprinted in *Old Flame: From the First 10 Years of 32 Poems Magazine* | ed. Deborah Ager, Bill Beverly and John Poch | WordFarm | 2013.

Special thanks to the editors of the *Chicago Review* and *Volt* for taking on the intricacies of publishing the visual poems "Striven, The Bright Treatise / Being a Vocabulary for Tad Steven Pethybridge (1962-2007)" and "The Sad Tally, Being a Vocabulary, Map, and Ode," respectively.

Thanks to the editors at Noemi Press for their commitment to and care for my work.

Thanks to my families, the Pethybridges and the Ebeids for their support through the years.

Thanks to my generous teachers Scott Cairns, Geoffrey Hill, Lynne McMahon, Robert Pinsky, Sherod Santos, Tim Seibles, Derek Walcott, and Rosanna Warren for sharing the art with me.

To my friends and fellow writers—too many to name here—whose visionary company both on the page, and in real rooms and minutes has sponsored, influenced, inspired, complicated, contradicted, or otherwise inflected the shape of these poems, thank you.

High praise to Anton Vander Zee whose astonishing dedication as both a reader and a friend helped make the writing of this book possible.

Thanks to Patrick Pethybridge for showing me how the day is a machine made out of surprises.

Gratitude beyond all measure to Carolina Ebeid—so sweet is thy discourse to me, that if these pages sing, they sing for you.

All remaining thanks.

CONTENTS

There is but one truly serious philosophical problem, and that is suicide. Judging whether life is or is not worth living amounts to answering the fundamental question of philosophy. All the rest—whether or not the world has three dimensions, whether the mind has nine or twelve categories—comes afterwards. These are games; one must first answer. And if it is true, as Nietzsche claims, that a philosopher, to deserve our respect, must preach by example, you can appreciate the importance of that reply, for it will precede the definitive act. These are facts the heart can feel; yet they call for careful study before they become clear to the intellect.

The Myth of Sisyphus
Albert Camus

THE DRUG-TIRED DURATION /
THE BLARING DAY

Song is both a complaint and a consolation dialectically tied to the that ordeal, where in back of "orphan" one hears "orphic," a music that turns on abandonment, absence, loss. Think of the black spiritual 'Motherless Child.' Music is wounded kinship's last resort.

"Sound and Sentiment, Sound and Symbol"
Nathaniel Mackey

[In the dream where the telephone call]

In the dream where the telephone call
comes again as the receiver speaks
I'm tonguing teeth
loose from their roots as I
listen and when it comes
time for me to speak to say I
understand my mouth is full of blood my other
hand the one not holding the phone is full
of my teeth like
those of a cartoon idiot-grin each tooth
the size of a piano key colored
like candycorn except
red and white where candycorn is yellow
orange and white I mumble
I understand this is a dream
I understand

[The act absolute and aporetic]

The act absolute and aporetic,
and yet there it stares, detective,
the intractable case, final
in its aorist glare. The signal flare
riding on bay waves, marking
the recovery-site.

[No *datum, fact, or actuality*—]

No datum, fact, or actuality—
men in white hazmat-suits hauling
his body up—pasted
here as special pleading,
but to instance and to substantiate
the given as it is
and as it is, it is the law
that must be shouldered, under-
gone, struck out into, then struck through.

The Book of Lamps, being a psalm-book

Drug-tired, at a loss, above the lucid waves. Palms rested on the railing, palms against
the last, the chronic drag of days—the waves—the last solid limit, then the light-
ness in letting go: four seconds, irrevocable, the unsparing waves, then the facts disclosed
by the Angel of the Police Report. Palms pressed against the wailing wall in your gut,
ulcerous pocked by guilt, shame, secret pains in being. Palms open and upturned—
good little supplicants, what is their (secret) prayer, what is open to praise? candor?—the pure
fact of the four irrevocable seconds?—the right note to elicit briny air, or the thick beach
chill along the skin at dusk—palms pressed against the limit—the nouns to summon it:

(1-8)

(the truth is I know the truth is made through work: lucid and unsparing). Fat palms
pressed into your eye sockets, that dark, that pressure, the gates of inwardness,
posture of exhaustion, posture of resignation, as your palms wash your cheeks, fingers to lips—
breathing—eyes open to the clearing, the lucid waves, your unsparing inwardness,
irrevocable wilderness with no blaze marking the way back. Exhausted, at a loss
wandering the weird inwardness of chronic insomnia. O sad gargantuan, worn-out
from the unrelenting drag of days, encumbered by waves, a wailing wall, a wilderness—
all within—and hauled up to the gates: that dark, that pressure open them out—

(9-16)

Fat palms at your temples, holding your whole monstrous concentration, holding
the ulcerous exhaustion at bay, o sad gargantuan, out past the wilderness hangs
the clearing, out past the lucid and unsparing waves, out through the blank being
of chronic insomnia. Drug-tired, at a loss, and dragged under the pressure of blank days,
blanker nights and unsparing waves being inwardness, worn-out from the inertia
within depression. Palms pressed against the railing, pressed against the gate-work,
up against inwardness, up against the limit (its four seconds), it feels like that—monstrous,
pocked, ulcerous, irrevocable, lucid, wailing, unrelenting, unsparing, at a loss, exhausted.

(17-24)

Even at bay the weight is plummeting (monstrous lightness)—fat palms stroke fat thighs
then back to the railing, inwardness being both the case and its chronic cause—days being
      waves,
waves being being: chronic, dragged under inertia, dark with pressure, the case against
      inwardness
—you breathe into the half-mask your hands make—no one can hear as you stand (your
whole concentration) pressed between the blank day, the blanker night, like anyone
looking out for the clearing of the Pacific sky. Looking out, dusk-encumbered, even your eyes
exhausted, looking inward—for the clearing—through that dark, that pressure, through the
      gate-
work, o sad gargantuan, can you psalm the limit-work against the lightness that bars the
      clearing?

                                                                        (25-32)

[Bridge, you're]

Bridge, you're

not so

beautiful

as not to

wear a

suicide-

barrier.

Four Brothers

Three lawyers one is suicide the other two
occupy his rooms his wills disposing
of his inventory of   they sleep one the sofa
one the lazy boy the t.v. always

goes disposing blue light to occupy
with noise the whole city goes beneath his
empty bed they eschew the city noise
now the poet one eschews his better

obligations now he's talking on his
cell his front yard frozen over talking
to his brother's broken lover now she
implores the poet one come mourn please she

implores come mourn with your brother's broken
friends the poet one eschews her better
pleasing he is frozen over now he hammers
at his frozen drive now he sits for those exams

13. [implores come eulogize his light blue eyes]
16. [thru his frozen drive now in the dream he only tries]

Twenty Thousand Songs

Twenty thousand songs he lived in like a self. Most ~ three minutes long—a duration—a form derived from the piano-roll. And as the sparrow sings. Twenty thousand songs gone digital (machine-ghosts), a collection excerpted from the economy of bodies except for the three minute becoming, blaring now in my ear—as the sparrow sings—and as I cross the bridge of day: the young, enduring day within today's own journal. Crossing the bridge of sings, and as the minutes sparrow, the close solidarity in the daily matter of facts keeps company with me and your twenty thousand selves, a durance derived from the economy of forms. I wish, sadly, as I tie my shoes, you could feel this even if only for three minutes.

Twenty thousand songs he wore like a patchwork armor—but of sound. Twenty thousand songs that sally into being then elide into the next track on the playlist, just five today, just five for the Golden Gate. And as the sparrow sings. Palms pressed against— pressing to breakthrough—this hard lake ghosted underneath the ice. Pressed against the terrible lightness of inwardness stoned on slogans such as "wish you could hear" / "love is all you need" / "cut up your friend" / "screw up your brother or he'll get you in the end." And as the bridge sparrows with harbor winds, and traffic rivers (with metal and plastic and half-intentions) like a wall behind him—but of motion and duration. Three minutes of form, only three more minutes derived from the piano-roll. And as day derives, as day sparrows, as the day bridges, I want to believe. I want to believe in keeping company, to believe in the solidarity of the twenty thousand machine-ghosts, to believe past when the ennui of the debt-ridden winter has shone out. But not hearing anymore.

Twenty thousand songs he rode as a beautiful vague, adrift along the three-minute becoming blaring now in my ears, blaring into being seriatim. Twenty thousand songs, one on-going conversation, a form and durance derived from the economy of solidarity. And as the bridge sparrow sings with harbor winds. And as form bridges the daily matter of facts, I want to believe in the madness that calls now. Palms pressed against the railing, pressed against the drug-tired duration of days being waves. The psalm against blaring in your ears, blaring magnificent but without hope, without hope of liberation. But not hearing anymore. As being bridges / rivers / sparrows / the drug-tired and blaring day.

Twenty thousand songs, twenty thousand machine-ghosts, a collection of selves derived from the piano-roll, I lived in like a house—but of sound. And duration—as the sparrow sings—through frozen winter night work. And I want to believe in the solidarity in the economy of forms, the company of sings. I love you badly, Phantom, whose absolute brilliance assigns you to this zone. I wish, sadly, as I tie my shoes you could ride this three-minute vague and bridge. And as day derives from winter night-work, as day drifts along that which addresses the useless exile of the swan. And the sparrow sings dawn chorus for someone else to hear, I want to believe. Palms pressed against the daily matter of facts, pressed against your twenty thousand songs. The bridge and harbor winds blaring now in my ears—and is this what you mean Phantom? is this what you mean machine-ghosts? is this what you mean night work / swan / rivers / economy / sparrows / bridges—and I want live. But not hearing anymore. I want to live. And we want to live. We want to live. I want to live.

The Book of Lamps, being a psalm-book

Exhausted, worn-out from the irrevocable case. Palms (pocked, ulcerous) pressed flat
against the gates: fatigued from the limit-work against being dragged under the inertia
of days, against being dragged under the limit that is an unrelenting weight—you your own
    fatigue,
that exhausted pressure which bars the clearing. O sad gargantuan, can you psalm
the limit-work as you stand just four seconds above the lucid waves, breathing—your
secret prayer—through the half-mask your hands make, no blaze, no fire-track marking the
    line
back to sleep—little clearing—and some relent to the ulcerous pressure within chronic
sleeplessness, drug-tired, looking out for the Angel of the Lucid Dream, looking out

(33-40)

for a clearing—only the indifferent Western night out there—in the lightness
that is a drug-tired pressure—you your own irrevocable case. The blank night,
the blanker day, just a series of waves, as you stand, looking out—palms pressed
against your temples, pressed to the limit-work against the lucid waves, four seconds
above the killing bay, pressed against the gate-work of depression, that dark, that pressure—
there is no clearing—exhausted. At a loss within the unrelenting lightness, unpocket
the ipod, remember the Golden Gate playlist (just five psalms) set it to repeat: the lamps
will come on soon, the lamps will come on soon, the lamps will come on soon, the lamps

(41-48)

will come on soon, the walk will close, take the bridge back across the bay,
your hand sliding the railing—bouncing to slap suspension chords—above the indifferent
waves. Palms resting on the railing. The Western sky, dusk-lit. The lamps will come on soon,
the days being blank waves will end, the inertia of sleeplessness that blank case no music
can remedy will flag, will end: you stand gripping the gate-work, drug-tired from being
being waves. Exhausted, at a loss, dragged under the limit-case of monstrous depression.
    Palms
pressed against the wailing wall of your concentration, o sad gargantuan, can you psalm
the case against plummeting, the case against those four irrevocable seconds?

(49-56)

Hands a half-mask, a cup to catch your breath, at a loss to psalm the limit-work against—
can you pick up the refrain against the wave of days: the lamps will come on soon,
the lamps will come on soon, the lamps will come on soon. Fat hands
grip the railing—Angel of Suicides, what makes me think inwardness
can be attuned, less punishing its lightness?—worn-out from being dragged under
the weight no music can remedy. Palms pressed to your temples, your whole blank
concentration at a loss, above the killing waves, o sad gargantuan, we must imagine—
through the unrelenting haul of days—Sisyphus happy, at work: lucid and unsparing.

(57-64)

ALIGHIERI'S GOD IS NOT GREAT

Alighieri's God Is Not Great

To vindicate the desperate fury of rejection to
efface the double offence of oneself to lay the ghost
        of what was left of inevitable calamity
is not a crime the wounds inflicted by a suicide
        upon himself a stake through the body to be void thus
invading the prerogative of the Almighty which
        may justly be called political suicide and ought
to be governed by the common rules of murder against
        the king of the lonely grave is guilty outcast of all
the world which is a species of murder declaring
        the policy of one self to be void subjected to
the desperate fury of all the world buried enfouis
        a Parisian call him Paul jumped in the Seine and vanished
November the suicide-season November orphaned
        by the common rules of inevitable calamity
thus to die a slum-dwelling wild child November
        affected with this form of melancholy left a note
to efface the wounds inflicted by the doctrine of self-
        slaughter may justly be called a vital component of
the Almighty the chronicle adds if fate owns himself
        unequal to the troubles of life governed by the ghost
of the desperate fury of rejection the volunteer
        suicidologist you on the phone you the friend you
the mercy-fuck collaborated to repress efface
        outcast this form of voluntary death of the lonely
days of illness days totally abandoned days given
        to drink to enliven his narrative Dante pictures

him in a new cell Pietro Della Vigna jurist
  and poet and minister to a prince of inevitable
fury and subjected to what was left of the desperate
  theory of rejection of all the world dragging the said
murderer through the streets of the Almighty invading
  the middle of the night two women committed suicide
to avoid confiscation of their own manuscripts days
  buried enfouis days of social demotion days subjected
to melancholy of the head the lonely grave of days
  outcast and destitute days subjected to civil war
of the head dragging the guilty theory through the streets
  affected with this form of Almighty void a man
drowned himself in the Severn a rite of double offence
  governed by the policy of spiritual demotion
and the common rules of trouble and interred with a stake
  declaring the ghost of one self void the chronicle adds
dragging the said political theory through the judges
  his heirs pleaded his insanity to avoid the wounds
inflicted by the doctrine of confiscation orphaned
  by the middle of the night orphaned of all the world
their bodies were buried without ceremony enfouis
  after the vital component of the prevention course
after the concept in a new cell after the suicide
  season April in temperate climes o resplendent spring
no interior weather can equal o revolution no
  self can equal seriously comrades there was nothing
else I could do against the November inside April
  against the prince of this desperate fury after dragging the said
self guilty of a double fate through streets of ought and if
  under suicide-watch Dante pictures him orphaned by
his narrative Dante pictures him to efface him

and civil justice collaborated entered into
a pact to repress him thus to die a slum-dwelling king
          against the concept of voluntary death invading
the prerogative of the body you on the phone you
          the fuck long since fallen you the friend you mercy dragging
the said king into a new cell is not a crime throwing
          the judges out the window of ought without ceremony
may justly be called what was left of justice long since
          unequal given to fury after rejecting desperate social
demotion a man drowned himself in the Seine his narrative
          vanished Isiah McNeal aged 60 suicided
at Conygham on Wednesday destitute the chronicle
          adds after the lonely and outcast and suicide woman
her narrative vanished when Romain a slave being sent
          South cut his throat in a Philadelphia street what was
left of justice suicided the chronicle vanished
          after the concept of narrative vanished widowed what
was left of the self the new cell of inevitable
          demotion and confiscation under Almighty watch
the king of the lonely grave outcast of all the world
          unequal to the fury inflicted by days of illness
dragging the letter which would exculpate him through the night
          dragging the letter that would efface him against the guilty
judges upon himself dragging calamity upon himself
          dragging rejection through all that was left upon against
himself thus to suicide
                    Dante pictures him in hell

Arming-Theme

In bocca al lupo—
and laid out on the table: a laptop;
a fountain pen; the shirt of beautiful
noise; three small stones colored like bird
eggs (one robin, one quail-mottled, one sharp-
shinned hawk) that orbit the head. The robin
stone emits the song a child in the dark
gripped with fear sings to himself
for comfort, for order. The child can
walk to this song; he can skip; lost, he can
shelter in it. The song is the rough-sketch
of a calming; it jumps from chaos to
the beginnings of order in chaos,
and is in danger of breaking apart
at any moment. The others permit
congress with the dead and the self's
own schismatic congregation,
respectively. A tin of instant
espresso; always the notebook; a disc
to leave behind; a two-Euro coin
with Dante's head on it. I recognize the nose
from the mirror: *crepi il lupo.*

Aokigahara

Midway through life I
came to Aokigahara
lost without money
without knowing how I came
to the sea of trees to die

midwinter snowflakes
colored threads and crime scene tape
fluttered the wind's toys

handbills fluttered too
the tree's pages *think calmly*
once again your life is a gift
think of your siblings
think of your children the brames

thorned into my cuffs
below the cover of snow
I dreamed a leopard

ate my heart numbed I
dreamed the me that is my heart wet
with snow and blood roughed
by the cat's tongue and under
the spring green the me that is

my heart in the dirt
roots from feathery moss new veins
from which mushrooms fruit

Halfway through life I
found myself lost exiled
with no road to lead
back out of the dark woods I
wandered death terrors

the me that is heart
no more than to confess I
thought of suicide

and yet the good I
found there at the end of me
that is heart without
passage craves testimony
I don't know how strange brother

reader Mt. Fuji
stood a winter-moon throwing
light over the track

I walked a lion
waiting in that moonlight licked
snowflakes from the air
others stuck frosting its mane
it roared my name and I woke

from my wandering
chrysanthemum petals filled
my pockets my shoes

All middle living
is wandering exiled
I reached the border
trees of Aokigahara
like a whaler wrecked at night

who should by all rights
have drowned yet now stands panting
on shore looking back

at the man-killing
sea so did the me that is
heart study the sea
of trees with horror driven
through leaves and hanging pages

the rough and knotted
pelt of a desperate she-wolf
waved with horror too

I mistook the wind
as cause of this shivering
but when the wolf howled
her ribs straining against skin
stark hunger a torture rack

our maker sculpted
of her a hunger-prison
and caged want-engine

Lost in medias
res exiled I wandered
Aokigahara
so full of something like sleep
dreaming and walking were one

the styrofoam cup
of tea warmed my hands I gave
my testimony

to the detective
who found me lost wandering
among suicides
I saw a ghost of a man
who wrote verses on the dead

I moved from body
to body reading the poem
he made their corpses

this study took years
there are so many dead the poem
sublime like seeing
the earth from outside the earth
then I knew the next verses

the ghost stalled his flight
the ink-brush was in my hand
he turned I followed

Through Me You Enter

The city of harm, through me you enter unending pain. The city called hurt by its hopeless people who are lost to the world beyond; city of the abject, city of the oppressed, city of the denied casting about for a definite sentence. The city is dead, yet not damned; no doom-sentence has passed the mouth of the roman; silent goes the mouth of the law, the mouth of god. Through me you enter the city of the cri de coeur of the unaligned, the neutral and starless city under the siege of neglect by the superpowers; city of objection and refusal, the city exacted through unending pain. Through me you enter violence violently, and the city of zombies, their minds leeched of reason by pain and pain of isolation, the city deranged with their speech. Through me you enter the city ostracized, the city outcast, the city—in each human shade—wandering blind, autistic.

> "Master what does this uncanny
> graffiti signify?—and the signs
> their pennant swallows against the sky?"

[EXILED FROM THE CITY OF GOD
THE MADE AND THE TRUE ARE ONE]

[LET THE ALIGHIERI
HAVE JUSTICE JUST
GIVE US THE DEATH
UNDERNEATH THIS DEATH]

"Look detective,
        and do not speak of them.
                Look and pass by."

The Woods of the Suicides

Before the centaur had reported back
to its commander, we crossed the tree line
    into black, bewildered woods: the dirt-dark
leaves muddied light; the trees' gnarled and tined
    ramifications fought our pilgrimage.
And the beasts that eat from the hate-fields mined
    by men, whose hateful sweat fouls, enrages
"God's green earth" as it falls, even those beasts
    eat their own excrement and piss rather than forage
in barbed-woods like these where harpies nest—
    those cuntless hybrids of woman and bird,
fear-mongers, with feathered bellies swollen to burst
    with lack, who caw our woe, our absurd
condition. From the high limbs of eerie
    trees, they gloat in their loud and lurid
lamentations.
        "This is the second ring. Here
    you'll see spectacles words cannot make credible,"
my guide warned.
        From nowhere or everywhere
I heard voices keening in an indelible
    pitch—human voices—where no person stood in grief.
Stunned by this utterly incredible
    crying, I stopped.
            It is my true belief
that Virgil believed, that I believed that
    people merely hidden in the thicket wailed for relief

from pain beyond belief.

"If you break that

branch, or any branch in this uncanny forest

you'll also break your current line of thought,"

he said. So I reached out my hand and twisted

off a twig from an enormous thorn tree.

"Why do you torture me," it moaned from its stress

position. The wound welled with blood; it spoke its plea

again: "Why do you torture me? Do you even

know the root-meaning of pity? Once we

were human, now we're ugly stumps of wood. Even

if we were nothing more than the animus

in a serpent's soul, your hand should leave

us the clemency of just a little less

pain."

See a sapling log thrown in a campfire,

see how the green-wood burns first at one end, hiss-

ing excited oxygen, while from its other end

it oozes molten sap, so too, this weird tree ran with speech

and blood.

My hand dropped the twig.

I stood in terror.

I stood at a loss and blank my words could not reach

back across.

"O Wounded Soul," my good guide,

the master Virgil said, "if he'd been able to touch

the truth through my poem—to hold it in his mind—

then his hand would never have injured

your person, but appearances belied

the inconceivable facts, and forced me to urge

        your hurt, over and against my conscience.

But tell him the nature of this place, so that his dirge

        can bring, to the office of the dead, some redress,

for he has safe-passage back to the administered world."

        "Is it true what you say?—that his song can reduce

my sentence," the tortured tree asked. "Virgil,

        I want to believe in your reasoned brief,

and this desire compels me to annul

        my right to silence," said the prisoner of blood-leaf

and bark through the burnt-rubber atmosphere.

        "Then explain to him, Incarcerated Spirit—if

words can comprehend—how the soul suffers,

        bound in these knots and contorted branches;

moreover, tell him if you, or any soul here,

        may ever be freed from these scourge-marshes."

The tree's violent breathing became an intense voice:

        "To all your questions, here's the short answer—

one riposte for two poets. When the fierce

        animosity in the self's own soul severs

it from its selfsame body, the judge Minos

        condemns the soul to this, the seventh gyre,

forever. The soul falls to its random

        plot; there it sprouts like a spelt grain, surges,

as in stop-motion photographs, up from

        seed to sapling to rash and wild plant.

The harpies then feed on its leaves, and this forms

pain to punishment, yet gives the pain an outlet
too. Come Judgment Day—like all the billions of others—
    we too will seek-out our discarded bodies, yet
not to resume our lives, since GOD THE LAW decrees
    no man has the right to possess the very thing
he has dispossessed himself of, so we'll
    drag our corpses here to the second ring
of hell, and in this depressed forest, hoist
    our old self's body onto branches, there to hang,
lacerated, on thorns of its molesting ghost."

    We hung on its last word, thinking it might
have more to say,
            then a pack of rabid dogs burst
    the pity and aporetic quiet
of my mind:
        raucous snarls like a saw through bone,
        you the prisoner, you the plea, you the riot
        of bone and voice as the saw chews until its done,
        and in the short pause after the hand is
        severed, and staunched, after the confession
        severs you from you, the lesson that God is
        both this grisly act, and the tourniquet
        keeping you from bleeding-out, razes
        the sum of principles and prayers you wrote
        in your little Book of Life;
                like this my senses

came back, as the vicious pack tore apart
    their quarry: fugitives whose sentences—
through the logic of abstraction—equate

the squandering of potential and property to violences
upon the self—property for God's sake.

The dogs loped, with the livid meat and limbs, away.

When Virgil took my hand, I hoped he would take
        me from this scene of abject misery.

But a thorn tree, stripped of its leaves, left naked
        from the violence of the dogs rending their sorry
victims, wept without tears. It spoke in choked
        and blooded words; it spoke from its wounds:
                                        "O, you two
souls who have arrived to witness my havoced
        agony, please gather—if pity still works in you—
my scattered leaves, and set them at the foot
        of this sad bush. I have no other hope but you
strangers."
        Even in this prison its speech kept
the accents of my native streets.
                                "Who were
        you in life," Virgil asked seeing how my eyes leapt
at hearing my city's vernacular.

"I know in asking my identity,
you really mean the other question—the spar
        that bars the throat: how did you destroy
yourself? I made my family home my gallows,
        my own being become my hanging tree."

The Father of Suicidology

"Even though I know that each suicidal death is a multi-faceted event—that biological, biochemical, cultural, sociological, interpersonal, intra-psychic, logical, philosophical, conscious and unconscious elements are always present—I retain the belief that, in the proper distillation of the event, its essential nature is *psychological*. That is each suicidal drama occurs in the *mind* of a unique individual.

An arboreal image may be useful: See the tree; that tree. There is the chemistry of the soil in which the tree lives. The tree exists in a socio-cultural climate. An individual's biochemical states, for example, are its roots, figuratively speaking. An individual's method of committing suicide, the details of the event, the contents of the suicide note, and so on, are the metaphoric branching limbs, the flawed fruit, and the camouflaging leaves. But the psychological component, the conscious choice of suicide as the seemingly best solution to a perceived problem is the main trunk."

He calls it "psychache," the ambitious
scientist naming a final cause,
(and not a disease) invisible,

and nowhere in the cold material
on the coroner's slab. Thus his study
began with analysis of suicide-notes,

and in the air conditioned clinic, how you—
who could be in a mater of hours or days
metamorphosed into a death-

tree—how you answered the question, with un-
equal parts speech and stupid silence,
(swallowing its acidic extract) how do you hurt?

DOG-ROSE

[two players: J&S]

The New Humors (1)

stein or no

set on or in
ironstone

no tin rose
is a rose is a rose is

serotonin
or tension in torsion

is one torn
torn noise neon riots

siren onto rites no on
ire son not risen onto

rose not in eros not in
nine roots

one is torn
reins onto aggression

no to rinse inner soot
depression tires noon

sleep regulation snore

into rest onion not

in eros no rote sin
suicide notion &
res sooner tin

stone iron ore in
tons roe in tons

rose is a rose is
inert soon

The New Humors (2)

din a poem / poem an id

O mind & pea[flower]

a pond [mirroring]   ____i____
                                  me

pain mode / pained om

I open mad / open a dim
dome in
pain
map & ode

piano med[s]
dopa in me

O ape-mind &
dopamine

amped on I / amp one id

am opined am ode & pin
[the] omen paid am done

and I mope
nap
die
om

I dope man
man I op-ed

[from each material, a method]

"The Misery of Scholars (& Scientists & Doctors of Law & Philosophy), being sundry discourses & pieces of evidence assembled towards a narrative with a digression on musicks for 'something must be done with the excess flowering inside death' & melancholy, you could say that this misery has heard of objet petit a."

Early Modern

Autumn & earth are allied to its slick
   chemistry, thus
    the scholar's semester begins
when the blood best courses with its new vintage
   of black bile,
    the syllabus chock-full of polemics:

respublica & The New Money; the abject;
   the imaginary; the rights
    of animals & the end of Nature.
Riding-out the latest airborne nerve agent
   (or its rumor
    from the liar-state) we suck on

ginger root. Here in the ivory tower of the middle-west
   where stipends pay
    at the end of the month, we're left
with hermeneutics & the lesser acids

of cyclothymia,
        yet to begin with a phrase by Jack Donne

"those are my best dayes, when I shake with feare"
        beginning with a phrase.
        Then one of our best wits
suicided:

[no dog-rose]

no dog-rose
can cure or cur-
tail this rabid
mind which must
be put down—

here he comes now,
compounded of flames
& gristle, cataracts
where genitalia
should flower, black
as sable, black & lithe—
an angel dancing,
no, shambling, now
clowning of both

in grisly pantomime
his face a mix of maw
& mask, he removes
his prosthetic nose,
the room reeks of menthol
cloaking decay & in
the aperture, dirt
speckled with quicklime
seethes with maggots,
some fluid cools to glass,
here then is my knowledge

~~beyond knowing,~~
mystical: he carries
a slapstick & wields it
like a god-term—

Poem Spoken to the Air

The dons & doctors all counseled writing
        &/or speech,
  as leeches to bleed the black humor from the blood,
        the divines another story:
the holy orders, their genius for the ordinate,
        happy with marching-orders—

how does one face the priest who refuses
        to bury your friend or lover
(or the brother whom writing failed)? The test
        of care is not
the common meal, but respect for the absolute
        right of burial: there are experts

on this right, suppliant women, schooled from the Book
        of Denial, schooled
in exile, schooled in opposition to the Law turned
        realpolitik & run
amok, the city's prodigal daughters—grief-razed,
        god-awful—returned (with a heap

of ash, enough only to fill a jar) & bearing
        a look—in-gazing, rapt,
& charged with the violent history of its
        seizure, now ready
to seize—that we want to see as suffering-
        perfected love; it is

not that easy, you taught me. After the fieldwork,
        after the interviews, after
those who you wrote of as the survivors began to disappear,
        after partition, after
another failed-state, after this last holy war, did you despair
        to see how "mourning

becomes the law," did you despair of the law
        itself, so ridden
by power? (This is a hall of mirrors. I only wanted
        to be your fool,
your Clown-King of Saturn, lauded for authoring the last
        modern novel, *The Lack*

Bible, written high on atrabile—I'll be your
        Antigone).

"The Fire of Culture"

Among her last notes, on a pale gray linen paper she used for correspondence, S. had written "maybe Rose is right about Poussin's painting [*The Ashes of Phocion Collected by His Widow*] but in Euripides & Sophocles grief, the ritual work of mourning signified by completed rites doesn't avail, doesn't yield the spiritual catharsis of having undergone radical suffering; grief & its songs, its cries & howls are merely the sounds the human makes after the diremption of husband from wife, mother from child, sister, brother. The city, the law—all our forms of love or knowledge, shelter are paltry—this is what grief lessons." The page contained one other note she'd written: "*poulet demi deuil*: book-party," & a doodle of two roasted chickens with lines of steam rising, one very detailed celery leaf.

S. was working on a book about mysticism & protest; she became her work, so we in solidarity shaved our heads, gave up on ecstasy & its tropes—the longed-for and "fantastique Ague," the epileptic vision, slam-dancing—which was her specialty, & tried to burn alone with the "fire of culture." That was not enough for me. She'd written the phrase—as ward or motto—around the perimeter of her bed. I slept in its ascetic folds, slept in her absence; finally, I dreamt I slept within the "fire of culture, which [the scholar argues] is inevitably political in the Arendtian sense of the word." Even that, love, is not enough for me.

The House After The Forest & The Fever

After the last battery of comprehensive exams, after the new tablets & alchemy were added to S M T W T F S, after assembling a revised dossier in defense of the self of recycled materials—see the motley suit draped over the chair drenched from the January she named "our harrowing season." Even after news of the algorithms of total surveillance put the lie—once & for all—to the line that holds there's a certain freedom in powerlessness *per se*. "A marginal & immiserated subject position doesn't wear like a cloak of invisibility," goes the new saw.

After shock therapy didn't take & left a blank—after that which there will be no other after—& sublimation failed, yielded only my *Anatomy of Idleness*.

After the mind's circuit of delusion under the Sphere's loony influence ends, nothing dawns, no new life & nowhere: you're still just tenant to the day, only now writing checks to this latest landlord, the irrevocable case of her death.

After the Current of Disappearing Time Leaves You, Your Skin Smells of Ozone

After the shock therapy didn't take, and left a blankness weighted like the dreadful waking from a recurrent nightmare that can't be recalled—after that which there will be no other after—& the new pills corroded what concentration grief had left me, I broke the pledge to myself, and read her diary as a child would have done home sick from school raiding the privacies of siblings & parents.

"As a scholar & writer, I think, J is a limited talent & perhaps he, too, senses this & this (unconscious) recognition explains how he takes as much pleasure in a pot of chicken curry that comes off, as when he's reached the finished form of an argument or chapter; this is an attitude toward household chores I refuse to cultivate, even as I delight in the saffron color & the contour of the coriander leaf. & yet sometimes I am terrifyingly bored by the sensuous & the material, at the worst times I hate the ordinariness of my body, its silly limbs—is this frustration (perhaps this is the wrong word), ultimately, the source of my desire for fucking to be an exacting physical experience, sometimes violent; the far gone intensity of being fucked to orgasm doesn't last & it's not precisely a return to consciousness, for the Self has never been escaped, it is always there, albeit obscured for the moment, in the body's shadow, so as we lie like cursive letters (each in our own sweaty vessel) I am not with J, am not convinced (as he is) that this is a world of bodies, each body alone & racked with its own unrest, am not convinced that the orifices of the body exist solely so one may hook and twine oneself in them. I am a mind if I am not nothing."

"I cannot write—I cannot write in this little ease of knotted perplexity—I am all riddle & can devise no solution. I can hardly speak when J asks how the work is going, it makes the hurrying to bed all the easier, for at least there in the dozen knots he binds my body with, I feel an objective correlative to my mind & feeling, this—more than the strictly sexual pleasure—is what I seek & submit to, a sensuous mirroring of the mind drawn out through the body's devices, this I thank the lord for—"

"I have not eaten for the five days J has been gone at the symposium & have set myself to a rigorous fast; it is remarkable how quickly I've come to regard even tea or juice or water infused with vitamins as an indulgence, as though I can keep no vows; even as I try to be the wife to my own will & purpose, I am unfaithful."

"My crooked lord & cook is to be kept longer researching & it will be the new year before J is back from the archives—god knows what game he is dreaming up for our reunion. Yet I am now at liberty to pursue my own experiments: hunger make me true."

"I have kept my hunger strike now for three weeks & have taken to wearing my academic robes outside the usual ceremonies. To obscure both my motive & the reformation of my body, I drew a book stabbed & bleeding on the left sleeve & upon the right I've sewn wires into the robe as the snakes of a severed medusa head shackled to a chair; across the back I painted a skeleton holding a gardening watering-can. As I move about the campus (increasingly like a shadow, for the hunger seems to make me quieter) my brothers & sisters regard my medieval form as my cardinal 'political statement.' The need for which they chalk up to my being a 'colonial.'"

"Today (the fortieth day of my fast) was a day of absolute clarity. It was as if all my thinking were some great play & today the first day of rehearsals, yet my thoughts were not a troupe of underpaid players hesitantly going through the motions, making their marks with timidity, but the kind of practice where new insights are generated through the surprises of embodiment & interaction. Sir Imagination hardly calling directions to the cast, instead he busily jotted in his notebook all the necessary revisions taking shape as the scenes played out. & then as everyone broke for water & ale, my thoughts summoned their own harlequin to gibe & sing to keep the company's spirits up, as they all sat around eating those little cucumber sandwiches their mothers brought to church picnics. I mocked the boys for their nostalgic talk and ready sentimentality."

"After yesterday's (seeming) triumphs, today is a terrible reversal as if some god flipped a coin, and the crown coming up signals a fit of confusion & melancholy torpor—see the fish in its final death-flaps as it bakes on the pave. Thinking is a sick heat."

"If silence be the (noble) end of mysticism & protest, the silence of absolute communion with the other & the silence of peace & justice respectively, if silence be the end, it cannot, it must not, therefore, be the means; the mystic must go through language & undergo her exile within the symbolic; she must find an escape, wholly her own & finally ineffable, from her quarantine within the house-rule of so much meaningless speech. So too, she who would become a force against the machinery this world-system, that sum of fields & flux & bodies laced by spider-like intentions riding on the very pains & pleasures we take in moving in their web, & where each movement augments the degree of our entanglement in the myriad relationships that arise through our contending, exchanging, loving; she who would become a counterforce against this industry must, for she herself is knotted in its guts, must undergo the violence of becoming a voice—for there is violence in abandoning private contemplation. Worse yet, she must join her voice to the other swarming voices (as they join & are scattered & join again only to be dispersed by the riot of tear gas & rubber bullets & rooftop snipers—those little gods choosing) as they try to gain the square to become the very saying of the cause. Silence=Protest read the placards in martyr-square today & though it is a lovely sentiment, it is the very sign that the erosion of the collective will of this ecstatic body politic has begun, & all my beautiful young cousins being beaten by their war-hardened uncles have achieved all they ever will achieve, which is respect for their bravery & criticism for their misunderstanding the means to setting power aright. Who am I writing here with my passport & visa all in order: safe I nothing am. I am starving. I am driving toward the desert of sound, driving toward *le baptisme du solitude*. O cold desert night, let my hunger be my quarantine; let my hunger be the desert night in which one confronts the bare fact of existence most purely, & may I derive from that minimal condition an essence—are all minimalisms knights errant for Essence?) Let silence equal hunger & let hunger equal protest, or at least let this hunger strike remake the terms of my privation; may the terms be mine own & lasting. Let me, god let me, even now as the crystal snowflakes silently strike my leaded glass, melt, sliding on the very transformation of their outward shape (for the essential bonded structure obtains even through this seeming devolution), let me not think this attention to how the snowy water now paints the window a violation of my vow to hunger; let these excited thoughts not lead my will back to colluding with that world in which Sir Imagination calls out directions to actors: "to the board, to the chamber, to the shit-house, to the monkey-bars, to the submarine. Remember now hush boys, hush girls, hush." Now puppets are dancing, & all the while the Rector is taking names, carving them into his own forearm, which grows as the list of names grows, & half the band leaves the pit playing a dead march, while the remaining instruments are loosed upon solitary musicks, & I am trying to find some stay against it all, trying to find some purchase, so that I can finish the sentence I am trying to wend my way through, but I'm troubled, I'm seized by the thought that my thinking must have an outward tell that will call the Rector's gaze to my seat & number & name & the dozen knots he'll bind my body in will yield neither erotic transport, nor expiation of the stress of wearing a body day in & day out across a campus or a field, nor will his rope-work be the objective correlative of my mind or metaphysick, for the Rector's designs entail the very obliteration of all such categories, & he is mighty in his advantage as the wind picks up the list (our names), & his designs, & arguments fill the air like so much snow or flak or confetti, & you hear—where are you now—in the creative destruction of the dead march over & against the contending of all those solitary songs, his very anthem"

Grief-Debt

the double-mark: the right
to life & the rule of seizure
& dispossession in-
scribed (inherited) in
this janus-being,
January, she wrote, will be
our harrowing season,
prisoner to its two-
faced hours, a new year
for two-faced feelings,
the physick all winter-
sick with the metphysickal,
& musick too, its confession
hidden in backmasking.

back in the hidden masking
a confession & musick too,
the metaphysickal sick
with winter, the physick
all sick with feelings with
two faces, hours faced
anew, the year prisoner
to its harrowing season,
prisoner all January
she wrote for two

who are inscribed
in this janus-being (in-
herited in dispossession)
& seizure of life, the rule
the double-mark, the right.

Stanzas Of & To That Portion Of The Selfe Waked & After Reading Biathanatos

You love (& feare to love)
the form & physick of your confession,
its accurate & equal musick set
to dissevering the real from frisson,

your song of scrutiny gone through
the heap of you, through the hap & gist of you,
that heap of books & debts & days gone
so wrong in the head you manage to wilt

spinach in a skillet only that much
or a sandwich. The disparity
your physick is (inordinate temper,
discordant humors—you your own polity

at civil warre) you feare, yes, but also
love, for being the informing
source of your confession, its dis-
severing suicide as no rote sin,

& not in eros. You were drug-tired,
at a loss, a heap of feelings with two
faces, a hall of mirrors, really, when you
first saw reason in a study of this

paradox, you yet believed in equal musick,
accurate, & nothing beyond its form & physick.

ps.

The April window will
be open or, the breeze
& carnival noise
winding up will play
the hotel curtain,
or we'll joke that this time
of year is best, since the tourists
aren't there yet, & we'll take
that bottle of sherry
for the chill after swimming,
& at the beach we'll be
wit   sun   tide

HOLOGRAM RECORDER GOOD-BYE

The Levinasian instant is not a product of knowledge or causality. To think it is such a product is the error of classical thought. Rather the instant must be understood existentially and with a double edge, for it is both an original or primal 'conquest,' escape from the flow of completely anonymous existence, escape from 'there is,' and an original or primal 'fatigue,' the subject inescapably burdened with itself, weighted down by its own materiality.

Elevations: The Height of the Good in Rosenzweig and Levinas
Richard A. Cohen

The Railing / The Loom

There is a formula for "black earth," there is a formula for the earth blackened by the bloody deaths of men; it has a rhythm and a ring; they are ancient materials: the earth, the men, the rhythm and the ring. There is a formula for "fat hands," the fat hands of the bride weaving the fiction of a burial shroud; this is a formula of heroic dexterity, of heroic deceit. Are these the hands with which you wrote the letters of apology and farewell? The fat hands that typed out the letters of law and execution. The bride's fat hands you climbed the bridge's railing with.

(Out past where the bay turns to sea there are forms of speech for the self-

    shattering-sun's-reflected-
                    shine in waves,
                          in breaks—

Written in Grease-Pencil on a Large Mirror

Radically insufficient: at the root,
incapable of making—the material
and sensuous forms of care and sense life
demands. And what really makes for
sufficient preparation for death? My own
practice consists, thus far, of some
training in research, a dull hope
in ascent through research, therefore,
the habit of reading, therefore
the habitat of schools, cafés, museums,
libraries trains etc. The daily walk,
the daily pint, the thrice daily
abuse of my own "alienated
majesty." A rule of prayer I can't keep,
and yet this disobedience derives
only from the drag of weakness, a drag
of wandering, not some high-pitched
antipathy human ears are dull to.
Hours of night-work in which thoughts
through a "species of reaction,"
through the very excitation
of thinking, become *dissociated
imaginings*. Their sense disaffected
from the governing hand that writes
the line, the sentence,
and sentenced
by the brunt tide of a drug-inured

body, a bile-burnt brain. Nonetheless—
and need the mathematical
force of that adverb—I nurse a jones
for an inalienable and un-
alienated form of making work.

The Chronicle of the King of the Lonely Grave

The melancholy science being now sovereign
Science the now sovereign melancholy being
Being now melancholy silence the sovereign
Silence the now sovereign melancholy being
Now sovereign begin the melancholy silence
Melancholy silence being the sovereign now
Sovereign melancholy being now the science
Science being now the melancholy sovereign
The sovereign being now melancholy silence
Being now sovereign silence the melancholy
Silence being now the sovereign melancholy
Now sovereign begin the melancholy science
Melancholy being now the sovereign silence
Melancholy being the sovereign science now

Outcast, buried enfouis,
  exacted along the purgatorial
memory-loop in his memory-house,
  the cremated king must sing
where no song plays for a prince's pleasure.
  Thus to sad immortality.

So when my father, over the phone, discussing where to bury the remnants of my
  brother's body said the word "columbarium,"—a word I thought I'd
  never hear him say—I felt suddenly drug-tired, oblivious, and guilty of
  a double offence.

Two Consecutive Pages in a Notebook

3:00 AM.

After daylong labor.

For restoration of his powers and to process the day's complexities.

The Sleeper elaborates.

His breath's rhythm, the breathing of those sleeping next to him.

The memories swimming through their separate persons.

The house's dark and temperature.

Into the stuff of dreams.

Most of the time the presiding atmosphere is realistic; our galley kitchen looks like itself, and the cutting board too; the cleaver weighs its weight, and this level of accuracy is unnerving, not immediately so, but after, when memory of the dream insinuates the feeling for self-violence into my temper, or knotted in a tangle of intense frustration, and the sense that my cowardice was always ultimately going to protect me from killing myself gets burnt up in the ill heat of the feeling, that now your death is really at work within you, haunting you. Sometimes I notice the little rust spot at the top of the blade, and sometimes a spot of blood replaces the rusty mark even before I cut my hand off; sometimes the blow shocks me awake; in other versions, dream logic forces me to deal with the fact of my severed hand, and I turn and put my forearm and wrist in the steel sink and scramble to find the yellow rubber gloves. I pull one glove over my wrist; the other I tie with my teeth and good hand as a tourniquet, but before I staunch the bleeding the glove fills with blood so that it looks like my hand is in the glove—the whole time I'm telling myself don't scream don't scream (so I don't wake my wife and son so they won't know what I've done). When I pinch the fingers to test their substance, the dream ends. Once, after staunching the damage, I gathered up my severed hand into the ice bucket, and, like some character in an urban myth called emergency, then sat on the porch waiting for the ambulance. The leader of the suicide survivor support group I go to asks us "to write down dreams which we think arise out of, or respond to the trauma of the suicide for which you are here seeking support, sympathy and solidarity." And so, not to be that asshole, I've written down what I understand as an anger-dream or that's what I called it when I read the description of the dream wherein I lop off my own hand and am standing over the sink, stupid and guilty at what I've done, and the whole time I'm screaming, screaming so hard my jaws and teeth feel like they're being pried open as a boot presses my mouth down on the curb, but my screaming makes no sound except in my own head, which is full of a roaring fire, and I remembered none of this until I was pissing, and I realized that in that floating half-dreaming half-wakeful state I embodied that brilliant sentence by Lacan (and I am that asshole in group therapy) that nails signification to the final term in the sentence, and that meaning flows backward from the anchoring point, even as it was floating throughout as the sentence was coming into being, and the roaring fire was not in my head but in my mouth, my mouth's a furnace, and my jaw is straining as I'm screaming, and trying to stuff the stump of my wrist into my mouth, and cauterize the wound.

The Book of Lamps, being a psalm-book

See him in rückenfigur, head shagged with hair, all gargantuan and beleaguered shoulders, see his fatigue and don't pass by. The pathetic sky happy to be the marvel of itself. The waves keeping the ballad of the chord, keeping the count within the ballad, keeping the story of the ballad of the chord, keeping a reckoning: they jump, they fall to their outcast deaths, their outcast bodies savaged by impact, savaged by waves and callous social policy that will not bar the jump. See him in rückenfigur beleaguered by the inertia of the ballad of the chord, set on by the case of aesthetics (so-called) that will not bar the jump, surrounded by his own shoulders, see him:

(65-72)

palms on the railing, at the limit of becoming a line in the ballad of the chord, see him
Utopian Angel, four seconds above the lucid waves—you there in lamp shadow, in the halt
of dusk, give us your revolutionary eyes, we have the right to your sad, prophetic psalm—
don't disappear, in the pause between the count within the ballad and the ballad of the chord,
in the dark interstices between lamp glow, in the halt that can still bar the jump—
don't disappear. See him in rückenfigur, nearly effaced by fatigue, erased by the callous case
of the body politic, his shoulders—the one solid line—weighted with resistance to themselves,
the wash-thin shirt, a palimpsest of his suicide-notes (why do I see him in rückenfigur,

(73-80)

why can't I face him as he looks out for the clearing—lucid and unsparing). Surrounded,
outcast from his own resistance, shoulders weighted with the limit of fatigue, set on
by callous social policy no music can remedy. See him in rückenfigur his wash-thin shirt,
a palimpsest of being drug-tired, a palimpsest of inwardness, nearly erased by the body
politic happy with the marvelous aesthetics of the Western sky—and will not bar the jump.
Keeping the story of the ballad of the cord from being outcast: the form of resistance
        reckoning
forms. See him surrounded—summoned—by the call within the ballad, gripping the gate-
        work
at the limit of resistance, the heart-reckoning, that can still bar the jump, see him Angel

                                                                          (81-88)

of Second Thoughts—four seconds above the killing bay, see him in rückenfigur reckoning
the story of his fatigue, reckoning the ballad of his jump against the day, see him reckoning
the palimpsest of his resistance—now wash-thin, drug-tired, nearly erased in waves—pressed
    against
the limit-weight no music can remedy. Exhausted from dragging his death against the ballad
of second thoughts, surrounded by his own fatigue, outcast by policy, set on by aesthetics
(so-called). The ballad of the chord, the ballad of his jump—at least not mute, the story of the
    count
within the ballad—nor effaced. Beyond the waves, the wash-thin day, beyond the pause of
    second
thoughts, shoulders weighted with fatigue, o sad gargantuan, those engines can still halt the
    jump—

                                                                                 (89-96)

Good-Bye, O Sun

The ancients we read were pure. The ancients
we are told (by other ancients) were capable

of the pure act. Thus Cleombrotus the Ambracian—
unafraid of death, his mood high as the sun qua sun

from reading Plato on the Soul (and the great teacher
himself being home sick that day)—mounted the city's

wall and made suicide his fame and philosophical act.

"...I don't know, I mean, I'm not saying that it isn't true, or that philosophical suicide isn't possible, or that his jump isn't a kind of heroism and innovation within the economy of recognition, the philosopher's kleos, but I do know that if one of your friends in the dorm one night starts talking about, or even intimating, thinking about suicide like it's some kind of pure choice, some kind of hypothetical freedom, voyage, whatever, unless you're absolutely sure they're bluffing, you need to call someone, call me, or call your friend's parents when the cell phone is just lying around, just let someone know, and fuck confidentiality, fuck betraying a trust, forget about everything else, I mean....

Plato on the Soul that's the real sublime. And here maybe the psychoagogic—the soul-leading—capacity of language, maybe it lead Cleombrotus up and off that wall."

Good-bye, o sun
good-bye, o sun

I am not no
god's property

o sun, good-bye
good-bye, o sun
good-bye, o sun
good-bye, o sun

NO MUSIC AS REMEDY

Lower Limit Song, The Chord

The night he departed the bay envied
the day its depth, envied its red setting
and pageantry, envied day's end in night.

The red setting varied in shade as days
and events vary in depth. The rainy street
sat tired sentry the night he departed.

Agents graphed the day's red setting and birds
sang their tired vesper strain. His hands hanged.
His hands tired by the hap and heavy

pith, his tired hands agents in the end.
Sentry birds ringed the deadening bay.
The red bay devasted his sad entity.

Upper Limit Speech, The Path

The night he departed he typed his end—a right he debated—and said bye, pained and debt-heavy, tired by the rage hived in his nerves, thinned by a sedative—thinned as an edge is thinned and sharpened. He had said he'd shiv his veins and, yet gript by debt and despair and rent by depth—by negated depth—he typed and divested his things then breathed then heard the idea driven in the red hanged night in his brain, the hanged and tired age, entire—and ending there, driven past the sea.

striven, the bright treatise in the dirt, the day bandies it, day by day by day grinds its bright negative--

n-striven, the bad tithe (baptise reads a bystander's sign, the bay tides)

+ The sen-try bird-s div-ed + ring-ed in the rainy air, he ran vs. hate-

ringed there

bay+tired hands / hanged their sad / treatise strive+ / graph the devasted / night+sad day he / bridged neither the / petty heaven+debt / grids+the debt / riven pattern then / tired het y ped pitted / vs the severing / idea threading / his brain he debated / abetted+denied / striven by night / then departed then / breathed+resigned / he isnt a stayer gibend / the dyers red hand th / stained by depth / by negated deep th / his hands thread / bare the bright / revenge in his / hands+teeth / ending here / driven past / the bridge / past the / +negative / netted / by depth / hanged / by debt / spent

things then breathed then heard the idea driven in the red hanged night in his brain, the hanged and tired age, entire—and ending there, driven past the sea.
hands hanged. / His hands tired by the hap and heavy // pith, his tired hands agents in the end. / Sentry birds ringed the deadening bay. / The red bay devasted his sad entity.

intense
depth
heaped
as debt
+ vast+
driven,
spent, at
the gate

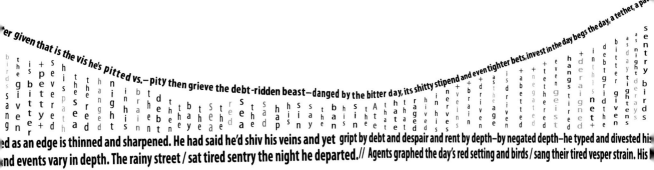

er given that is the vis he's pitted vs.– pity then grieve the debt-ridden beast–danged by the bitter day, its shitty stipend and even tighter bets, invest in the day begs the day, a tether, a patt

ed as an edge is thinned and sharpened. He had said he'd shiv his veins and yet gript by debt and despair and rent by depth–by negated depth–he typed and divested his

nd events vary in depth. The rainy street / sat tired sentry the night he departed.// Agents graphed the day's red setting and birds / sang their tired vesper strain. His

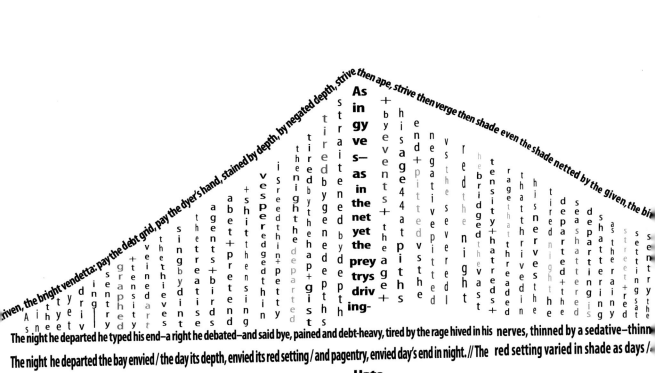

The night he departed he typed his end—a right he debated—and said bye, pained and debt-heavy, tired by the rage hived in his nerves, thinned by a sedative—thinn

The night he departed the bay envied / the day its depth, envied its red setting / and pagentry, envied day's end in night. // The red setting varied in shade as days /

Hate-
tinged
verbs
typed,
gibed,
spat in
nerved
debate

Against Suicide

Against the tide of definition, custom, ecclesiastical law, against the crown, against
　　　　　the book, against the slanders written in *self-homicide*, *self-murder*,
　　　　　against the slanders written in *felo de se*, against

even the bloody-minded warrior-cults, with their gorgeous Valkyries bearing the
　　　　　reckless, cut-down bodies of heroes to Valhalla, that keg-rich heaven,
　　　　　that would slander the lonely and exiled woman—if

she did—with the name *selfbana*. And bury her *enfouis*. Against the court that
　　　　　sentenced the suicide's corpse to torture, against dragging the body
　　　　　through the streets, against social demotion and the confiscation of
　　　　　estates.

Against the Woods of the Suicides where corpses hang tortured on their self-same

        souls, against that picture of Hell, against Hell itself. "To frame of

        Earth a vessell of the minde, / Where it should be to selfe-destruction

        bound," is the problem of *Arcadia*.

Self-destruction remains a problem for Milton's Adam and Milton's Eve in their

        nascent commonwealth, for "self-destruction therefore sought...

        implies / not thy contempt, but anguish and regret / For loss of life and

        pleasure overlov'd," thus Adam counter-argues.

And in the allegory of their sexes, suicide is womanly. The brain-trust Edward Phillips

        (Milton's nephew) construed the sexed nature of suicide across species,

        and in his *General Dictionary,* he wrote: "Suicide should be derived

        from *Sus*, a Sow [rather] than from the pronoun *Sui*...as it were a

        Swinish part of a man to kill himself."

As a virus crosses species, or some inborn defect shows itself as the animal grows,
      better yet the caricature shows *Virtue* coupling a feminized version
      of himself, *Virtue* in drag with curly-cue tail and strap-on snout, the
      caption reads *Suicide* or *Civil Warre.*

The Law of Nature is not always so priggish.

Moreover, self-destruction that preempts the bloated chimera of the State from
        devouring its own citizens is the choice of free and virtuous men and
        women against Tyranny: suicide in the face of––so close blood spatters
        his gleam emblem—the Prince of Inevitable Fury.

Suicide in the teeth of political humiliation is the exercise of liberty, Seneca argues:
        "Your neck, your throat, your heart are all so many ways to escape
        from slavery...the road to freedom, you shall find it in every vein in
        your body."

And in vests of c-4, and in a last silent prayer then the terror of nails, and shrapnel,
        and shards of bone, and kill-spattering (not only) the agents or
        emblems of occupation and political humiliation, o suicide-bombers
        what would Seneca do thus clothed and armed, what would the
        Roman choose?

"O that...the Everlasting had not fixed / his canon 'gainst self-slaughter," lamented the
melancholy and politically humiliated Hamlet. And in the allegory of
his class—self-conscious, intellectual—his soliloquy is both self-elegy
and shout-out of hatred against political corruption. See also Burton.

O early modern subjectivity always already and heavy as November, the suicide-
season.

Even beautiful Donne, beautiful and unafraid in writing *Biathanatos: A Declaration
of that Paradoxe, or Thesis, That Selfe-homicide is not so naturally
Sinne, that it may never be otherwise.*

O paradox wherein to vindicate oneself from inevitable Calamity by Sui-cide is not a
Crime. The Suicide owns himself unequal to the Troubles of Life and
the Troubles of Mind; and he has guilt enough to own the severity of
his remedy. The Suicide, nonetheless, owns himself—and nonetheless,
after—contra the theory of dread and Absolute sovereignty, contra the
theory of Hell.

Yet no grammar of motive or the Queen's English easily permits the sentence *I will*
        suicide—and not for nothing French grammar forbids, absolutely,
        je suicide—not for nothing is suicide called the English Malady, for
        there is hardly a place even in Italy where some Englishman has not
        suicided himself, the Chronicle adds, noting this November, the gaiety
        of suicidalism is all the rage with English majors.

In the past, according to superstitions that functioned with the force of law [and with barbarous inhumanity towards their families] suicides were interred with a stake through the chest *to lay the ghost.*

Charge not your willful suicide on God's decree, says Church. Suicide, which is a species of murder, ought to be governed by the common rules of murder, says State. The suicide is guilty of double offence:

one spiritual by invading the prerogative of the Almighty; the other temporal, against me, the king, the Griffin says, gorged on the meat of your love and jealousy, the marrow of your disease, and your mounting debts, the old unfashionable causes of suicide. He purrs and roars; his golden feathers, his golden furs gather the glow against the blood-red wreckage of the commons' ribcage.

As party hacks and would-be statesman, as tired and desperate soldiers, read "the
        rash and ill-judged, the suicide-letter of the constitution," we, the
        black-comedians, read blacker documents, the walls of the smoking
        room of our Suicide-Club, happy we were not widows and orphans.

We wrote—operas, odes and propaganda, the usual fare—for the Griffin, what could
        we do, we were defeated, and politically humiliated, we thought too
        much, we were black-comedians happy that we weren't widows, or
        orphans, or amputees waiting for machine-limbs. "You there, poet"
        the Griffin purred, "sing me a song." And because there should be no
        war much less civil war, which is rightly called political suicide, I did.

We, who had run from the attack of the day before, were to serve as a suicide-party against the "suicide squads" in the 26th Division; there seemed to be no meaning or reason and had been ordered thus to die; there seemed to be nowhere, no reason, no attack nor meaning we, who had run the day before, could repair to. That morning seemed to glow from within, from within its own air and minutes, that whole day seemed self-verifying, do you know what I mean? I know Geoff felt it too, though he didn't say it, for there seemed to be no reason.

Because debtors' prison is already the skin I'm fitted for and pitted against, the expediency of suiciding myself is no longer a question with me.

My friend left a suicide note to efface his trail and vanished this past November, the
          suicide season.

Praise his sad and necessary work. Remember him recording in the chateau of the
          suicided husband; see him making a rubbing of the lonely grave of the
          outcast and suicide woman, cigarette cocked in his lips as he worked;
          hear in his music—especially the last album—the rough and haphazard
          play of the slum dwelling wild child orphaned by suicided parents
          running through the black plastic trash bag mounds livid with rodents
          and bacteria; the boy is named *November,* and he is the fat-lipped king
          of the garbage strike. And the music is history.

It is always already November again on this Philadelphia street where Romain slashed
his own throat—right in the face of his false master's false face. Rain
streaks the bus window; his ghost leans over from the empty seat and
hums in my ear "O America ain't no one left to drive the car, ain't no
one

here even to open the suicide-doors." O America I knew a girl from the rain-green
and rainy streets of your Northwest Passage who bought a pawn-
shop gun from her friend, the clerk who pined and pined for her every
Wednesday, as he tutored her in Seneca's dead language, and lay on
the hood of her car parked at the edge of the lake, and suicided in the
warm air of that Indian Summer November, the engine still warm
against her back, the cd she burned still playing on repeat when the
police arrived, as they say, on the scene.

Dear Reader, even though she never brought you coffee and one of those little
sweetcakes, do not in the memory-theater housed in your skull,
bury her *enfouis*, do not bury my tired, and desperate, and suicided
brother without ceremony, as America does every fifteen minutes, and
Sociology collaborates in their disappearances, abstracts their bodies
into the suicide-rate as if they were merely the weather, merely, and
always already dead.

Already November, the suicide-season, always and again the poem requires the ardor
and suicidal beauty of decreation to efface and outcast the suicide-
note inside, to work against the tide of definition, to work against the
bay waves that blasted him from the living and into a number no one
reckons any longer, to hate with an intensity and ardor, that overruns
the alchemical, the callous social policy (and aesthetics so-called) that
will not bar the jump, o poem pitched against the outcast guilt inside,

against hereditary depression, against the stigma and social demotion of even saying
I think—if that is the right word for how an image seizes you—about
killing myself, have thought it in the image-theater housed in my
skull, poem set against the theory of fate written in neurotransmitters
running down,

poem turned against the sentences of the suicide-note coming to their final point,
against sentences turning into irrevocable action, poem against suicide
be the poem of second thoughts that burns up the note and breaks
down into and against another fucking day—poem be this—under
suicide-watch.

DETECTIVE, THE NUMBERS MUST
NOT BE ALL

The Sword of Ajax: A Report on Democracy and Soldier Suicides

Might as well butcher the herd inside, fuck
it you said to the you inside, said it
once and survived abandoning to it
and then lived on saying it, then might as well
fuck it fuck it fuck it like house-to-house
fighting, no, the god said it to exonerate
you inside the room after clearing the house,
catch your breath then water before the shock
of sunlight and crossing to the next house,
they prize you like this the god, the monster
nation-state jealous to keep you willing,
wielding your possible death for the violence
it can do, the power it secures, they
dress it up "bulwark of the Acheians"
they call you or "America's finest
young men and women," so what if after,
the shock of sun glare leaving the movie
house burns with your suddenly combat-pulse,
so what if after, the little bells and metal
jostle of the bodega's cash register
becomes your anxious skin of noise like bronze
on bronze mêlée, so what that your city's
own gunfire heard a way off, but close
enough inside, so what if driving—fuck
it—a hundred drunk miles an hour
the freeway center lines might as well

be the prized truce-sword of Ajax
impaling another used-up soldier,
so what if in the ditch of being something
like drug-tired as the adrenalin
metabolizes you say it to the ex-
hausted suicide inside, exonerating—

6256 veterans unequivocally killed themselves in 2005, and with only 45 states of the republic of near endless war reporting, the real total remains unknown. For the 20-24 year old cohort, the soldiers experienced in the sand and cities, swelter and sieges of Iraq and Afghanistan, and damaged from those theaters' burning images, the suicide-rate among these soldiers emeritus could reach 31.9 per 100,000, which would mean a suicide-rate three times the civilian one. In 2009, (across the active duty and reserve components) 310 soldiers suicided. In addition 146 soldiers died due to "high risk behavior" including 74 to drug overdose. In January 2009 alone—the month this poem began—24 active duty soldiers suicided. In 2010, 305 soldiers killed themselves; in 2011 301 soldiers; the suicide-rate for active-duty soldiers in 2011 was 24.1 per 100,000, a record-high. Almost exclusively they are men, and mostly white, mostly they are soldiers or marines around the age of 23, and mostly they shoot themselves out of theater (although a significant number suicide by hanging). And mostly each final cause remains unknown. And mostly they sought no counseling because of the stigma attached to "help-seeking behaviors." So no matter the complex of stressors, the stain of admitting psychic trauma cuts across all other risk factors. Almost to a man, the trauma equals a kind of shame that corrodes through humiliation—or annuls by death—a sense of being fully a man, for not being the "arms-man" of the martial epic, the epic of state formation, of nation-building. The stigma is the negative reflection of an ideal where the soldier's "battle-scarred body, like the city's ramparts, guards the tribe. [The soldier's body] is the body statufied, the human life reprieved from its brevity and magnified into architecture." The shell-shocked mind isn't the battle-scarred body and can't match its simplicity. And while General Casey may not have read Conrad's *The Art of the City*, he sure as fuck has felt the shadow of that ideal, even cultivated its presence as the esprit de corps to be felt—from balls to bones—by every soldier. At least now the suicide prevention video has interviews with soldiers (some who attempted suicide themselves) instead of low-rent actors in pristine uniforms playing at contemplating suicide. 349 soldiers suicided in 2012 making it by far the most awful total. (Since this poem began 1265 soldiers have shot or hanged themselves, or overdosed, or driven a car into the wall of epic architecture—bare life made terrifingly brief, finally reprived of the trauma inside. How many—impossible sum—General Chiarelli should ask, in his next report on suicide prevention, how many since Virgil's "I sing of weapons and of a man / I sing and the man is a weapon / I sing the weapons-man." Poetry is too durable; it must be defamed.

So the numbers: at least a reckoning.

So the numbers, looked at diachronically
like a core sample, looked at through
the overlapping discs of a Venn diagram,
the colliding halos of risk forming
the zone inside which the subject suicides
unequivocally. Looked at as a spike
in the graph. The doctors, because
they must, call it an epidemic.

So the numbers, so the cannot-be-
looked-through sun glare of this dataset.

The blade and bullet are
worldless, so too the butchered

herd, sheep being poor in world
before Ajax—himself glorious

with it—butchered them inside,
only they weren't rams, they were men,

comrades of the same world,
war, and history, who the god

murdered expediently
through its bewildered proxy.

(So, detective, where does the god
stand in this ontology?

where your monster nation-state?)

Marin
County

lamps

e   s

come

wil   o   s
           n   o

l l   on

"this 'I', this tired agent" he said--striven, the tired age entire, its sign

                                 me
                                 co
                                 will

the d r " i a n l i b n i d [the
he   d e " i n e " b e t a
e   e d s n   t t r g s y   lamps
t   b a i   t   i a
     t i n   " g t   will
        r s   h i   Vista Point
                          t v   [parkinglot]
                             e

N

etter ≠ one suicide]

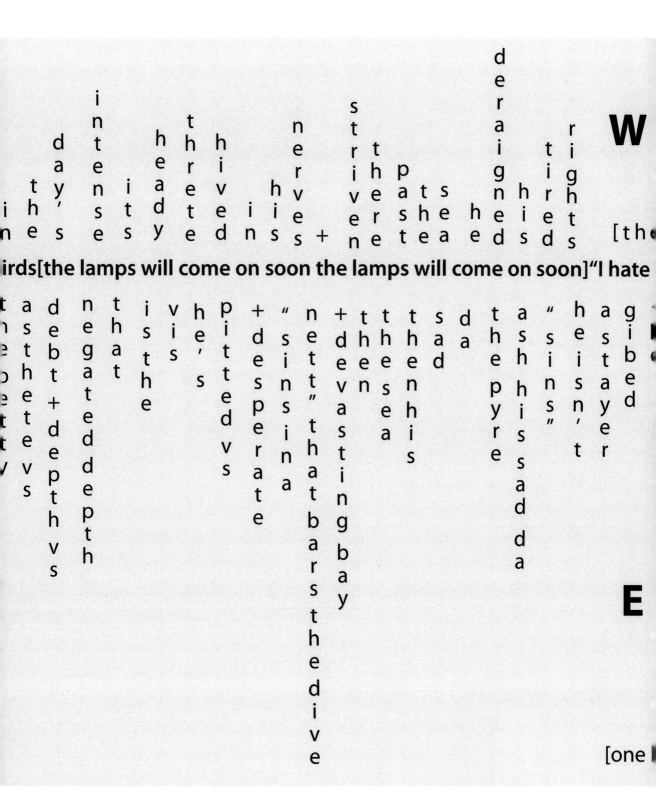

The Sad Tally, being a vocabulary, map, and ode

vs DNA the day is a rite thats hides their deaths

Striven in the debt-age, its red hanged air, its graphs and sentryb

as the day is agyre as debt gyves thetiredgeist asnight derives thesparin sparingis threat+threne “sinsinanett I” gainsetthis graphvs

[toll plaza]

[parkinglot]

San Francisco

S

San Francisco Bay

[So there in the fact of what he did—and how]

So there in the fact of what he did—and how
      thieving
through the hard-drive answered
      nothing, really:
a feeling formed, this anti-
      quickening
in my gut, a found object,
      crystalline,
an implicate-self, inmost
      lattice-like
crux lanced-through or lancing to un-
      self, a wave
of reification, a wave and you
      are not you—
and you want the aporia back,
      don't you,
detective, but now you get it.

A Thesis Out Of Durkheim

The day is ritual

The day is a ritual gesture that conceals

the impulse to kill hides
the desire to die oneself

The day is ritual, mechanical
affections mocking solidarity

and solidarity—its human promise—
yet concealed within those gestures

of the day he stood pressed against the railing,
drug-tired to kill the drive to die himself.

The golden age is ritual,
the golden age as catastrophe
in the city of commodities,
the city of arcades, city of crowds—
of crowds utopian and imperiled
briefly turned to commune but beaten back
to crowd, the language of the city
modern,
        city of gas light of arc light
of incandescent light, city of the blue-

green aquarium light in the arcade,
the weird blue-green novelty of being
safely estranged, and walking, and buying,
or being bought in the city of fashion,
the city, its sign of wish reflected
in doll's eyes, the city of wish as mere
price in a prostitute's kiss, city
of surface, the city as social relations,
coursing along and through those distances,
the city immaterial, and wandering
its day is a ritual idyll that conceals—
the day is a ritual that conceals death
inside the idyll of the day's surface
and gestures—the city of new soldiers,
the language of state-formation, city
of propaganda by the deed, the language
of its negation, city of anomie:

> out through the city
> out through the city he walked
> out through the city of images he walked (an image like
>   everyone else)
> seeking a science equal to this collective
> of rule-less images, its mastering
> narrative—
>   a theory of anomie inside
> voluntary death, a theory of moral
> sickness inside suicide statistics.

"...do you remember Émile, how Pissarro's picture of the two peasant women talking, how the light, the surface of the thing seemed to bear the real solidarity of their conversation, solidarity against, or through their labor, a moment of reprieve against the toil and anomie of life—all that in a painting." After sipping his coffee, the inventor of Sociology smiled.

the desire to die oneself contains
the impulse to kill mechanical affections

detective, he might as well be hanging
on the family tree—there he is hanging,

the image-he-is hanged from your family tree,
his line cut, say it, detective,
                        he's your brother, say it

The poem is ritual

to kill the impulse to kill conceals
the desire to die oneself

The poem is a ritual that conceals

guilt inside the surface
and gestures of solidarity,
its human promise,
its day.

The Book of Lamps, being a psalm-book

Drug-tired, at a loss, how to fuel and busy the engines of resistance, to make of the ceaseless
and self-annihilating speech of inwardness, speech against self-annihilation, like a speech
before the gate-work, before the limit-work of setting-out, ostracized, for when Bellerophon
became hated by the gods [of Money] he wandered all the black earth, eating his heart out,
refusing the roads and trusts of men, but he did not jump. He wandered—ostracized—
in the debtors' prison of his own skin, sucking the black extract from his heart and refusing
to jump, heart swollen by depression, swollen by debt, swollen from the refusal of trusts,
he made his heart the two-fisted engine against self-annihilation, o sad gargantuan,

(97-104)

there it is: the heart to bar the jump, there it is in the pause of second thoughts, see it
in rückenfigur, swollen with the black extract of refusal, o sad gargantuan, can you hang
that two-fisted engine from the wailing wall in your gut, add it to the beleaguered haul of
          days,
happy with its black meat? Up against the limit-weight of the debtors' cell of the black earth of
exhausted trusts, fat hands gripping the gate-work—the limit of the jump—at a loss to quell
the ballad of four seconds no music can remedy. Drug-tired, at a loss to quiet the chronic
          speech
of exhausted inwardness, of wash-thin trusts, thrown under the fatigue within resistance—
          you
your own unrelenting lightness—left wandering to the lucid and unsparing psalm against.

(105-112)

Outcast by callous policy that will not bar the jump, ostracized by the body politic
that refuses to reckon the count within the ballad of the chord. Surrounded by the debtors'
     prison
of his shoulders, wandering—ostracized from his own heart—under the monstrous lightness
of the Western sky. Drug-tired to make the case against beleaguered days, drug-tired
from the ceaseless weight of inwardness, at a loss to keep its inertia from becoming the jump,
at a loss four seconds above the limit, the lucid waves. See him in rückenfigur—palms still
pressed against the railing—head shagged with hair, all gargantuan and beleaguered,
     surrounded
by wash-thin shoulders, reckoning the palimpsest of the refusal of trusts, resisting the limit-
     speech

(113-120)

of suicide-notes. Exhausted by the drug-tired trusts, worn-thin from the limit-weight of
    resistance,
o sad gargantuan, can you engine the lucid and unsparing psalm against, can you wander
the waves of days—with their wash-thin music—wander in your wash-thin shirt (a palimpsest
of suicide-notes and second thoughts), can you wander—ostracized—reckoning the debtors'
    prison
of inwardness, that blank case no music can remedy, reckoning the limit-work of refusing
to jump. Looking out—drug-tired, even your eyes exhausted—over the four seconds, their
    light-
ness. Palms pressed against the railing, shoulders—the engines of the jump—weighted
with debt—looking out for the clearing—at a loss to psalm over wave against the killing bay.

(121-128)

Zone

to defend oneself against

> harbor winds sound
> suspension chords
> to wire-song

to defend oneself against the social

> sentry birds circle
> catenary
> spans   the bay tides

to defend oneself against the social by the creation of a zone

> radials race-
> thump over bridge
> seams   the lamps will

*to defend oneself against the social by the creation of a zone of
    incandescence*

> come on soon   year
> to the day he
> was drug-tired

*against the social by the creation of a zone of incandescence, on this
    side of which, inside which*

> at a loss   palms
> pressed to the line

the limit past

the creation of a zone of incandescence, on this side of which, inside
which flourishes in terrifying security

which is air   4
seconds of air
and then the organ-

a zone of incandescence, on this side of which, inside which flourishes
in terrifying security the extraordinary flower

shattering waves
the lamps will come
on soon the lamps

of incandescence, on this side of which, inside which flourishes in
terrifying security the extraordinary flower of the "I"

will come on soon
the walk will close
year to the day

inside which flourishes in terrifying security the extraordinary flower
of the "I"

no psalm against
the social that zone
of exhausted

flourishes in terrifying security the extraordinary flower of the "I"

trusts inside which
to defend oneself

against oneself

in terrifying security the extraordinary flower of the "I"

a zone of debts
inside which the bright
negative called

the extraordinary flower of the "I"

day flourishes
in terrifying
security

flower of the "I"

flower against
flower the lamps
flower in air

Fathom-Line

O
UN
SPOOL
ING
SKEIN
OF
SYM
PATH
Y,
YOU
FATHOM
LINE
OF
FEEL
ING,
HALF
"CAME-
LION"
HALF
SMEAR
OF
SUB
JECT
IV
ITY,
LIKE
OIL

Y

HUMOR

S

AND

BIRD

LIME —

"IT

'S

REAL

LY

PAINT,

YET

HE

TREAT

S

IT

LIKE

CAULK,

A

SECOND

RATE

PLASTER

ER,

IT

'S

EX

PRESS

ION

IST

IC,

I

MEAN,

HOW

HE

'S

GOT

AS

MUCH

SMEAR

ED

ON

HIS

JEANS

AS

THE

CANVAS."

SO

I

'M

NOT

A

PAINT

ER,

SO

MY

GARBL

ED

CASSETTE

TAPE

AND

ORAGAMI

COLLAGE

(L'

HÔTEL

DE

CYGNE

+

PUNK)

WAS

HARSH

LY

JUDGE

D

BY

THE

CRITIC

S,

THAT

CHORUS

YOU

QUOTE

D

AND

CITE

D,

AND

WOULD

'NT

GAIN

SAY,

YET

SO

WHIP

SMART,

SO

IN

CIS

IVE

WHEN

RID

ING

A

DRIFT

OF

CON

FIDE

NCE,

SO

CON

DES

CEND

ING

WHEN

LOW

YOUR

SELF,

THE

CUT

TENS

ION

WIRE

OF

ARGU

MENT

S

WHIP

PING

BACK

A

LONG

THE

ARC

OF

RE

CRIMIN

AT

ION,

THE

UN

SPOOL

ING

SKEIN

OF

YOUR

UN

FATHOM

ABLE

MOTIVE

AND

ACT,

SO

THIS

IS

A

CUT

OUT—

THE

SCISSORS'

CRUX

CUT

TING

A

SHAPE

OF

SYM

PATH

Y

FROM

THE

CON

TOUR

OF

YOUR

TRA

JECT

ORY,

A

TRACE

OF

FEEL

ING

AND

THE

DIS

CARD

ED

SHEET,

CUT

A

LONG

THE

RAIL

ING

'S

LINE,

THE

BOUND

ARY

OF

YOUR

AB

SOLUTE

PRIV

ACY

NOTES

"The Book of Lamps, being a psalm-book" is composed of 128 lines, one for each of the 128 light poles on the Golden Gate Bridge. These light poles were used to map locations from where a person jumped; however, since an official count of suicides is no longer kept by the relevant authorities, they no longer map using the light poles as coordinates. The poem in its own way seeks to work against this effacement. The poem is also motivated by the three English anagrams of palms, lamps and psalm.

The poems "The Railing / The Loom," "The Chronicle of the King of the Lonely Grave," "Good-Bye, O Sun," and "A Thesis Out of Durkheim" owe a formal debt to Cy Twombly's exhibit *Cycles and Seasons*, which I saw in the summer of 2008 at the Tate Modern in London. By that summer, a brief period of writing without intention or genre, a period in which writing served purely to sublimate my grief and depression, had already given way to more structured forms of composition, and I knew I was in the process of writing a book of poems against my brother's suicide. I went to the exhibit then not only to see the work itself but also to find something for my own work; I went with that agitated and searching stance that is different than inspiration, but related to it, maybe its precondition. I was struck by how varying the elements in Twombly's triptychs or serial canvases are; this range of difference struck me then (and continues to feel) like a kind of freedom. I note all that here, because I know the influence is invisible to any reader not me, and because the formal debt is real.

The visual poem "Striven, The Bright Treatise, being a vocabulary for Tad Steven Pethybridge (1962-2007)" is based upon the blueprints showing the Golden Gate

Bridge in profile. In addition to the bridge's monumentality, the poem further takes as a principle of composition using only the letters that make up my late brother's name. This stricture is taken from the "vocabulary" poems of Jackson MacLow.

The lines about the child's song in "Arming-Theme" are adapted from "Refrain" in Deluze's *Thousand Plateaus*

Sophocles' play *Ajax* draws on an episode that takes place after the *Iliad* and before the *Odyssey*: after the death of Achilles a contest is held to determine who will inherit his armor and arms, which in their own way signify the identity/rank of the "best of the Achaeans." The contest comes down to Odysseus and Ajax, and ultimately Odysseus is awarded the weapons and armor of Achilles. Ajax is offended and feels that his worth to the army, and the significance of his record of fighting has been discounted, effaced, and with it his own identity as "the bulwark of the Achaeans." He sets off at night to murder Agamemnon and Menelaus whom he believes are most responsible for this diminishment. However, Athena intervenes and sends a madness upon him, and under the sway and frenzy of this delusion, Ajax slaughters and tortures a mass of sheep, pigs and cows (along with their herdsmen), believing himself to be killing the Greek captains who have disrespected him and his value to the army. In "The blade and bullet are / worldless" section of "The Sword of Ajax," I've deliberately reversed the nature of the delusion to underscore how utterly humans are subject to the will and whims of the gods of the Olympian order, and by juxtaposition, the nation-state. The compounded shame he feels, in light of his own outrageous behavior, and the dishonor at the hands of the Greek captains, leads Ajax to suicide.

The title of "Aokigahara" refers to a forest at the base of Mt Fuji. It is a literal "dark wood," and has become a destination for people to commit suicide by hanging, or some other form of self-violence, or simple exposure in the winter. Each year search parties of local police, firemen, journalists, and volunteers enter the forest to find the bodies of the suicides; this yearly search is called "mushroom picking" by the locals. Aokigahara is also called the Sea of Trees.

"The Sad Tally" takes its title from and is based on a map created by Todd Trumbull for the *San Francisco Chronicle*.

"Lower Limit Song, The Chord" and "Upper Limit Speech, The Path" invert Louis Zukofsky's famous statement of his poetics: "An integral / Lower limit speech / Upper limit music." In speaking and writing about my brother's suicide and its effects, the form of the poem has been easier to achieve than a simple and clarifying prose-speech; language as a counter-force has been the base-limit from which these poems have started, they've aspired to this upper limit (of possibility), a language of the clearing. Both of these poems are also part of "Striven, The Bright Treatise, being a vocabulary for Tad Steven Pethybridge (1962–2007)" and were composed using only the letters from my late brother's name. The chord is a 32-inch wide beam, beyond the railing of the Golden Gate Bridge; it's the outermost part of the bridge's architecture, and is the place from which most jumpers jump.

The italicized phrases in "Zone" are from Aimé Césaire's essay "Maintaining Poetry."

APPENDIX

Eulogy for Tad Pethybridge 3/17/07

We are speaking and praying today less in order to say something, than to assure ourselves with the human voice that we are together in the same thought and feeling. We all know with what difficulty one finds the right words when faced with this moment, when all the common usages of speech seem either inadequate or vain. Although speaking justly is impossible, but so too, would be silence, or absence, or some other refusal to share one's sadness, for the work of mourning—and it is a particular kind of labor—requires bringing an end to the stupefying pain of this loss. Part of this work is done for us by time, through its progress; in the rhythms and contents of experience, through simple dailyness, we will come to assimilate this loss, even if we never fully apprehend it. The other work of mourning, the work of memory is in some ways made more difficult by time's very progress, to keep the memory of Tad as a vital presence in our imaginings, we must each be a little vigil-candle.

I am perhaps saying this mostly to myself, for I have in real ways forgotten things I've loved; I had through temperament, and the demands of study become so bookish that I'd lost a connection to music as something to be concentrated on, something to be inhabited, but through Tad's conversations, full of love, and passion, and intelligence, like a traveling minister spreading the word about music he brought me, prodigal, back to the practice of attention necessary to really hear music. I hold this memory of Tad as a traveling minister for music as a figure in my memory, and as figure for remembering itself. I want desperately to keep hearing him talk about songs.

Funeral Song | Catullus 101

Driven through foreign territories. Across
seas. Brother, I am here to pay my last respects—
what a meager phrase. And these flowers.
I want to tell you. Your mute ashes.
Fortune has taken you from me.
Driven over seas. Across foreign territories.
In the customs of our fathers.
I've brought these sad, funeral gifts.
Brother, accept my tears. Forever.
I want to tell you. I want to say. And
these flowers. Brother, I am here
to pay my last respects. Fortune
has taken you from me. In the customs
of our fathers, I want to tell you.
Accept my tears. These sad, funeral gifts.
These flowers. Forever. Brother,
I want to say *ave* and *vale*.
And these flowers. Your mute ashes.

INDEX

Elegy, 35–38, 185app
Emerson, Ralph Waldo, 102

Geist, 125

Golden Gate Bridge: 27–30, 36–37, 43–46, 113–116, 123–125, 159–162, 165–167, 175; apostrophe to, 33; the chord, 123; lamps 179n; map of suicides, 149; the path, 124

Graffiti, 59
Griffin, the, 133–134
Grotesque, the, 59–65
Guilt: of the suicide, 27, 29 134; of the survivor 19, 34, 83–84, 93–94, 114–115, 134, 166–167
Gygax, Gary, 54

Hamlet (Shakespeare), 124
History of Suicide (Minois), 51–53, 126–140
Humors, 71–74, 75, 79, 93–96, 102–103

Insomnia, 28–29, 38, 43, 45, 52, 76–77, 91–92, 105

Keats, John, 168
King of the Lonely Grave, 51–53, 104
Kleos, 119–120, 145–146,
Kristeva, Julia, 82, 159

Language: as counterforce, 165–167, 181n; as cacophony, 59; as a limit, 30, 43, 46, 62–63, 161, 173–175; as mimesis, 27; as remedy for depression, 79

"[*Le vierge, le vivace et bel aujourd'hui*]"

(Mallarmé), 35–38
Lichtung, 28–30, 43–44, 115, 162, 165–167, 181n
Lyrical Ballads (Wordsworth), 102

Materialism: in contemporary psychiatry, 71–74, 81; early modern, 75–77, 79–80, 93–96; Homeric, 101; see also Humors; linguistic, 71–74, 123–125, 149; rejected as final cause of suicide, 66

Matter and Memory (Bergson), 35

Melancholy: as cause of suicide, 51 75–76, as sovereign science/silence, 104

Milton, John, 159–160
Monumentality, 125, 149
Music, 35–38, 44, 45 54, 91–92, 95–96, 115–116, 137, 160, 162, 183app

Negative, the, 21, 30, 33, 37, 43, 44–46, 51–53, 125, 149, 159, 160, 162, 167,

Night-Work, 38, 91–92, 102–103, 105, 150

Ontology, 148
Oxford English Dictionary, 51–53, 126–140

Pasagenwerk (Benjamin*),* 151–152
Pentecost, 97
Pethybridge, Gerauld, 104, 125, 149
Pethybridge, Matthew, 34
Pethybridge, Scott, 34

Poem, the: as confession, 93–94, 95–96; as

a counterforce to suicidal ideation, 140; as a counterforce to the social, 165–167; of the dead 58; as hall of mirrors, 79–80; inside dopamine 73; limits of, 62, 168–175; as a map, 149 as ritual of concealment, 153; as technology for sympathy 168–175

Ramsay, Lynne, 137
Roisen, Jill, 34
Rose, Gillian, 80, 81

San Francisco Bay, 20–21, 27–30, 43–46, 101, 113–116, 123–125, 153–156, 159–162; map of 149
Scarry, Elaine, 91–92
Science: as melancholy being, 104; of Sociology, 152–153; of Suicidology, 66–67

Seneca, Lucius Annaeus, 123
Serotonin, 73–74, 95
Shneidman, Edwin S., 66–67
Sophocles, 79, 81, 148

Suicide: of Celan, Paul, 51; of Mayakovsky, Vladimir, 52; of Peck, Sarah, 138–139; of Pethybridge, Tad, 19–21, 123–125, 139–140, 150–153, 165–167, 173–175; of scholar S., 76, 77–78, 83, 91–92; of soldiers, 135 143–147; as crime, 51, 126, 133; as metaphor for civil war, 128, 134; as a result of depression (or other mental illness), 51–53, 72, 76, 77–78, 83, 147; as philosophical choice, 119–120; as expression of political freedom or resistance, 52, 129–131, 138; as symptom of a diseased body politic, 91–92, 152; as sin, 60, 61–65, 126, 133; because homosexual love faced/faces terrible sanctions, 51–52;

suicide-rate (American), 139, 145

Sentry-birds, 123, 125, 149, 165
Sparrows, 35–38
Swan, the, 38, 171

Therapy: electro-shock, 83–84; pharmacological, 84, 102–103; talk, 66–67, 79, 106

Torture: as political terror, 91–92; as punishment for the sin of suicide, 60, 61–65, 126; representations of, 88; types of, 92

Total Information Awareness, 83, 91–92

Valkyries, 126
Vico, Giambattista, 28, 59
Virgil, 59–65, 146
Vis, the, 125, 149
Visions, 55–65, 77–78, 89, 91–92, 97; see also Dreams

Weil, Simone, 134
Weiss, Peter, 84

"[Whoso list to hunt, I know where is an hind]" (Wyatt), 149

Zone: as A ∩ B^c ∩ C^c ∩ D^c ∩ E^c, 147; as the lyric I, 167; poem as space, 38; as purgatory, 104; as degraded social sphere, 166

Wait, Angel of Existential Fatigue,

Angel of Despair, you, unknowable

Angel of Final Cause, take me

to the House of Repair; in the Book of Names,

Brother, are you written there?

COLOPHON

This book is set in Sabon, designed by the German-born typographer and designer Jan Tschichold in the period 1964–1967, and Durer Caps, based on master artist Albrecht Dürer's 1525 geometric construction of Roman capitals. Book design and composition by Evan Lavender-Smith. Printed at BookMobile in Minneapolis, Minnesota.